Dear Parents,

Welcome to the Scholastic Reader series. We have taken over 80 years of experience with teachers, parents, and children and put it into a program that is designed to match your child's interests and skills.

Level 1—Short sentences and stories made up of words kids can sound out using their phonics skills and words that are important to remember.

Level 2—Longer sentences and stories with words kids need to know and new "big" words that they will want to know.

Level 3—From sentences to paragraphs to longer stories, these books have large "chunks" of texts and are made up of a rich vocabulary.

Level 4—First chapter books with more words and fewer pictures.

It is important that children learn to read well enough to succeed in school and beyond. Here are ideas for reading this book with your child:

- Look at the book together. Encourage your child to read the title and make a prediction about the story.
- Read the book together. Encourage your child to sound out words when appropriate. When your child struggles, you can help by providing the word.
- Encourage your child to retell the story. This is a great way to check for comprehension.
- Have your child take the fluency test on the last page to check progress.

Scholastic Readers are designed to support your child's efforts to learn how to read at every age and every stage. Enjoy helping your child learn to read and love to read.

—Francie Alexander
    Chief Education Officer
    Scholastic Education

For Hana, with much love
— M.B. and G.B.

Special thanks to Paul L. Sieswerda
of The New York Aquarium
for his expertise

Text copyright © 2001 by Melvin and Gilda Berger.
Fluency Activities copyright © 2003 Scholastic Inc.

Photography credits:
Cover: Tom McHugh/Photo Researchers, Inc.; page 1: Frank Krahmer/Bruce Coleman Inc.; page 3: Tom McHugh/Photo Researchers, Inc.; pages 4-5: E. R. Degginger/Photo Researchers, Inc.; page 6: Jack Couffer/Bruce Coleman Inc.; page 7: Stephen J. Krasemann/Photo Researchers, Inc.; page 8: Alan D. Carey/Photo Researchers, Inc.; page 9: Tom & Pat Leeson/Photo Researchers, Inc.; page 11: David Austen/ Stone; page 12: Robert Hermes/Photo Researchers, Inc.; page 13: Wendell Metzen/Bruce Coleman Inc.; page 14: Treat Davidson/Photo Researchers, Inc.; page 15: CC Lockwood/Photo Researchers, Inc.; page 16: Dr. Robert Potts Jr./Photo Researchers, Inc.; page 17: Wolfgang Bayer/Bruce Coleman Inc.; page 18: Nigel J. Dennis/Photo Researchers, Inc.; page 19 top: Roy Morsch/Bruce Coleman Inc.; page 19 bottom: Harold Hoffman/Photo Researchers, Inc.; page 20 top: Dr. Robert Potts Jr./Photo Researchers, Inc.; page 20 bottom: David T. Roberts/Nature's Images, Inc./Photo Researchers, Inc.; page 21: Bill Goulet/Bruce Coleman Inc.; pages 22-23: John Serrao/Photo Researchers, Inc.; page 24: James Prince/Photo Researchers, Inc.; page 25: Gary Retherford/Photo Researchers, Inc.; page 27: Charles V. Angelo/Photo Researchers, Inc.; page 28: Byron Jorjorian/Bruce Coleman Inc.; page 29: Stephen Cooper/Stone; page 30: Root/Okapia/PR/ Photo Researchers, Inc.; page 32: Laura Riley/Bruce Coleman Inc.; page 33: The Purcell Team/CORBIS; pages 34-35: Larry Allan/ Bruce Coleman Inc.; page 36: Frank Krahmer/Bruce Coleman Inc.; page 37: Gary Retherford/Photo Researchers, Inc.; page 38: Jeff Foott/Bruce Coleman Inc.; page 39 top: Bill Bachman/Photo Researchers, Inc.; page 39 bottom: Mary Beth Angelo/Photo Researchers, Inc.; page 40: Fritz Polking/Bruce Coleman Inc.

Library of Congress Cataloging-in-Publication Data is available.

ISBN: 0-439-31746-0

15 14 13 12 11 10   10 11 12/0
Printed in the U.S.A. 40 • First printing, November 2001

SNAP!

A Book About Alligators and Crocodiles

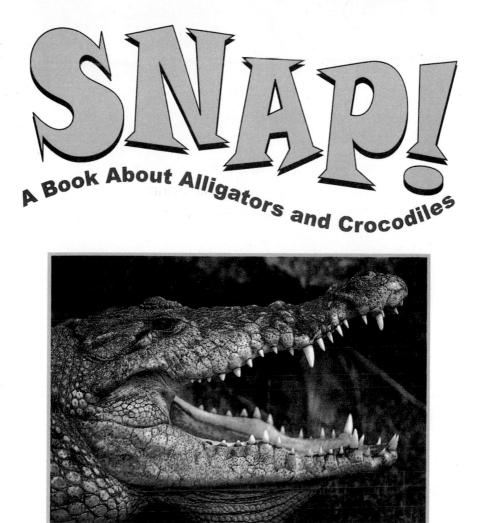

by **Melvin and Gilda Berger**

Scholastic Reader — Level 3

SCHOLASTIC INC. Cartwheel ·B·O·O·K·S· ®

New York Toronto London Auckland Sydney
Mexico City New Delhi Hong Kong Buenos Aires

CHAPTER 1
Lumpy and Bumpy

A giant alligator floats in the water.

You can hardly see its body.

Most of it is hidden.

You might think it's a lumpy, bumpy log.

Look carefully.

Can you spot the alligator's eyes?

They stick up above the water.

They let the alligator see all around.

The alligator's nostrils also stick up
above the water.
That's a very good thing.
The alligator can breathe and hide
under the water at the same time!

The alligator lies still.
It waits and watches.
In a while, a very large fish swims by.

Suddenly the alligator flings open its huge jaws.

SNAP!

It catches the fish with its many sharp teeth.
The fish tries to break free.
But the alligator holds on tightly.

Soon the fish stops wriggling.
The alligator juggles the fish around in its jaws.
It gets the fish into the right place for swallowing.
The alligator jerks back its head.
And the fish slides down its throat!

The alligator swims to the riverbank.
It slowly climbs out of the water.
It walks on its four short legs.
Its long tail drags behind.

Suppose you happened to walk by.
You might think the alligator is a crocodile.
The animals look much alike.

How can you tell an alligator from
a crocodile?

CHAPTER 2
Alike, but Different

The alligator has a long, lumpy,
bumpy body.
So does the crocodile.
The alligator has four short legs, sharp
teeth, and a long, strong tail.
So does the crocodile.

But alligators and crocodiles are not
exact look-alikes.
They have different noses, or snouts.

An alligator has a wide, rounded snout.
It looks like the letter U.
A crocodile's snout comes to a point.
It looks more like the letter V.

There is another important difference.
It is the fourth tooth on the bottom jaw.
In both animals, this tooth is extra long.
But the tooth fits inside the alligator's
upper jaw.
And it sticks up outside the crocodile's
jaw.

Crocodiles are usually longer than alligators.
They can also outswim alligators.
Most crocodiles weigh more, too.
That may be why crocodiles are better fighters.

Alligators and crocodiles often wait quietly for their dinner.
They lie hidden in the water.
They wait for animals they want to eat.

Both alligators and crocodiles live in lakes, swamps, and rivers.
But alligators live only in the southern United States or in China.
You can find crocodiles all over the world.

CHAPTER 3
Mothers and Babies

It's spring.
The alligators and crocodiles are starting
to build their nests.
The nests are on land.
But they are always near water.

The female alligator shovels with her
hind legs.
She scoops grass, twigs, and leaves into
a big heap.

Soon she has a huge nest.

It may be as big as a king-sized bed.

And it may be as tall as a first grader.

The alligator then crawls all over the nest.

She packs it down with her heavy body.

The crocodile usually makes a more
simple nest.

She just digs a hole in the sand.

Or, she makes a pile of twigs, grass,
and mud.

The female alligator or crocodile lays
from 20 to 60 eggs in her nest.
The eggs are white.
They look like the eggs you buy in
a store.
But they are bigger.

The female does not sit on the eggs.
The sun warms the nest.
And the female keeps guard.
She watches out for bears, skunks,
and lizards.
These are some of the animals that eat
alligator and crocodile eggs.

Sometimes an animal tries to steal
some eggs.
The mother attacks.
Most enemies will run away.
The mother's sharp teeth and powerful
jaws are very scary!

Two or three months pass.
The mother hears chirps from inside
the eggshells!
That tells her the eggs are ready
to hatch.
She digs the eggs out from the nest.
And she helps the babies break out
of their shells.

Sometimes the babies crawl into the mother's mouth.
She gently carries them to the water.
Then she opens her mouth.
Out they crawl.

A female alligator or crocodile seems to be a good mom.
She stays close to her babies for a year or more.
The mother protects her babies.
If an enemy comes close, she hisses or roars.

The mother gives her babies piggyback
rides.
She lets them sit on her head.
But she does not feed them.
The babies must find their own food.

Luckily for them, babies have full sets
of teeth.
The teeth are like tiny needles.
The babies use them to catch small fish,
tadpoles, flies, moths, and beetles.

The baby alligators and crocodiles grow
very quickly.
Some gain about a foot a year
for six years.
Suppose you grew that fast.
You'd be around seven feet tall!

CHAPTER 4
Day and Night

Alligators and crocodiles nap on and off
all day.
Sometimes they sleep in the water.
Other times they rest on riverbanks.

The alligators and crocodiles lie
in the sun.
Their thick skin collects the rays.
The sun warms their bodies.
Alligators and crocodiles are cold-blooded
animals.

Cold-blooded animals must get heat
from outside their bodies.
Without outside heat, the animals move
very slowly.

So, alligators and crocodiles live in warm
parts of the world.
And they bask in the sun.
When they get too hot, the animals head
for the shade.
Sometimes they go back into the water.

Alligators and crocodiles must look
for animals to eat.
These animals are called prey.
Fish, birds, turtles, frogs, and raccoons
are favorite prey.
So are large animals, such as pigs,
deer, dogs, sheep, and cows.

Suppose a crocodile spots a wildebeest (WILL-deh-beest) crossing a river.
The crocodile clamps its jaws down on its prey.
SNAP!
The wildebeest cannot escape.

Sometimes the crocodile grips the wildebeest in its jaws.
It drags the wildebeest under the water.
The wildebeest drowns.
Then, the crocodile tears it apart.
The crocodile swallows the pieces whole — without chewing!

Alligators and crocodiles usually eat their prey in the water.
Special flaps of skin keep the water out as they eat.
Other flaps cover their ears and nostrils.

Alligators and crocodiles also have extra eyelids.

They're like goggles.

They protect the animals' eyes underwater.

Yet, the animal can still see.

The teeth of alligators and crocodiles are special.

The front ones are very sharp.

The animals use them for catching and holding their prey.

The teeth in the back are short and blunt.

Alligators and crocodiles use them to get the food in place before swallowing.

Alligators and crocodiles lose many teeth.
Some get knocked out by their prey.
Others become worn and fall out.

Alligators may lose 3,000 teeth in a
lifetime!
But new teeth are growing in all the time.
One tooth falls out.
And a new one pops up to take its place!

Alligators and crocodiles look slow
and lazy.
But they swim very fast.
When chasing prey, an alligator or
crocodile can top 20 miles an hour.
That's almost five times the speed
of the fastest human swimmer!
On land they run only half as fast.

Believe it or not —
alligators and crocodiles have
good manners!
Let's say a crocodile catches a cow.
It tears off a chunk of flesh.
And it swims away to enjoy its meal.

Other crocodiles swim over.
They rip into the cow.
In a while, the first crocodile returns.
But it waits its turn to eat again!

Alligators and crocodiles do not eat
every day.
Once a week is more usual.
Some can go without food for as long
as two years!
How can they go so long without
eating?
They store lots of fat in their bodies.
Most of the fat ends up in their tails.

Chemicals in their stomachs break down
the food alligators and crocodiles eat.
This helps the animals digest what
they swallow.
Remember: Alligators and crocodiles
do not chew their food!

Alligators and crocodiles also swallow
pebbles.
It's not because pebbles taste good.
The pebbles weigh them down.
They help the animals float just under
the surface of the water and keep them
out of sight.

Some birds are safe around crocodiles.
Among them are white herons and plovers.
They often ride on top of alligators and
crocodiles.
The birds pick at tiny bugs they find there.

A plover may even hop into a crocodile's
mouth!
It acts like a toothpick.
The plover pecks out bits of food from
between the crocodile's teeth!
The plover gets something to eat.
And the crocodile gets a clean mouth.

CHAPTER 5
All in the Family

Alligators and crocodiles are cousins.
They belong to a family of animals called
crocodilians (krok-uh-DILL-yuns).
The crocodilian family also includes
gharials (GARE-ee-uhlz) and **caiman**
(KAY-mun).

Gharials are sometimes called **gavials**
(GAY-vee-uhlz).

They look most like crocodiles.

Gharials live only in Asia.

Caiman look more like alligators.
They live in warm parts of North and
South America.

Crocodilians are a very old family.
They lived at the time of the dinosaurs.
That was over 200 million years ago!

Today, there are two kinds of alligators —
the American alligator and the Chinese
alligator.
They live thousands of miles apart.
But they look very much alike.

The American alligator has a huge tail.
It is sometimes a powerful weapon.
One blow can kill a large enemy.
It can even kill a human being.

The Chinese alligator is smaller than the American alligator.
This animal is rare.
There are only about 500 left in the wild.

There are 12 different kinds of crocodiles.
The American crocodile lives mostly in Florida and Central America.
It is far less common than the American alligator.

The saltwater crocodile
of Asia and Australia
is the biggest of all
crocodilians.
One used to live in
Australia's National Zoo.
It weighed more than
one ton!

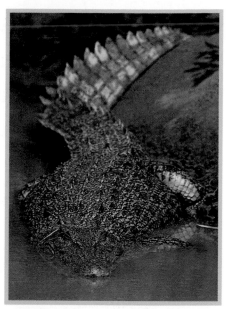

The Nile crocodile lives in Africa.
Some Africans call it "the animal that kills
while smiling."
Nile crocodiles actually harm more people
than lions do!

Crocodilians are amazing creatures.
Their ancestors walked with the
dinosaurs.
Dinosaurs died out millions of years ago.
Yet crocodilians are still here.
Let's hope they're here to stay!